T0068595

Daniel and the Silver Flute

United Synagogue Commission on
Jewish Education

Daniel and the Silver Flute

An Old Hassidic Tale

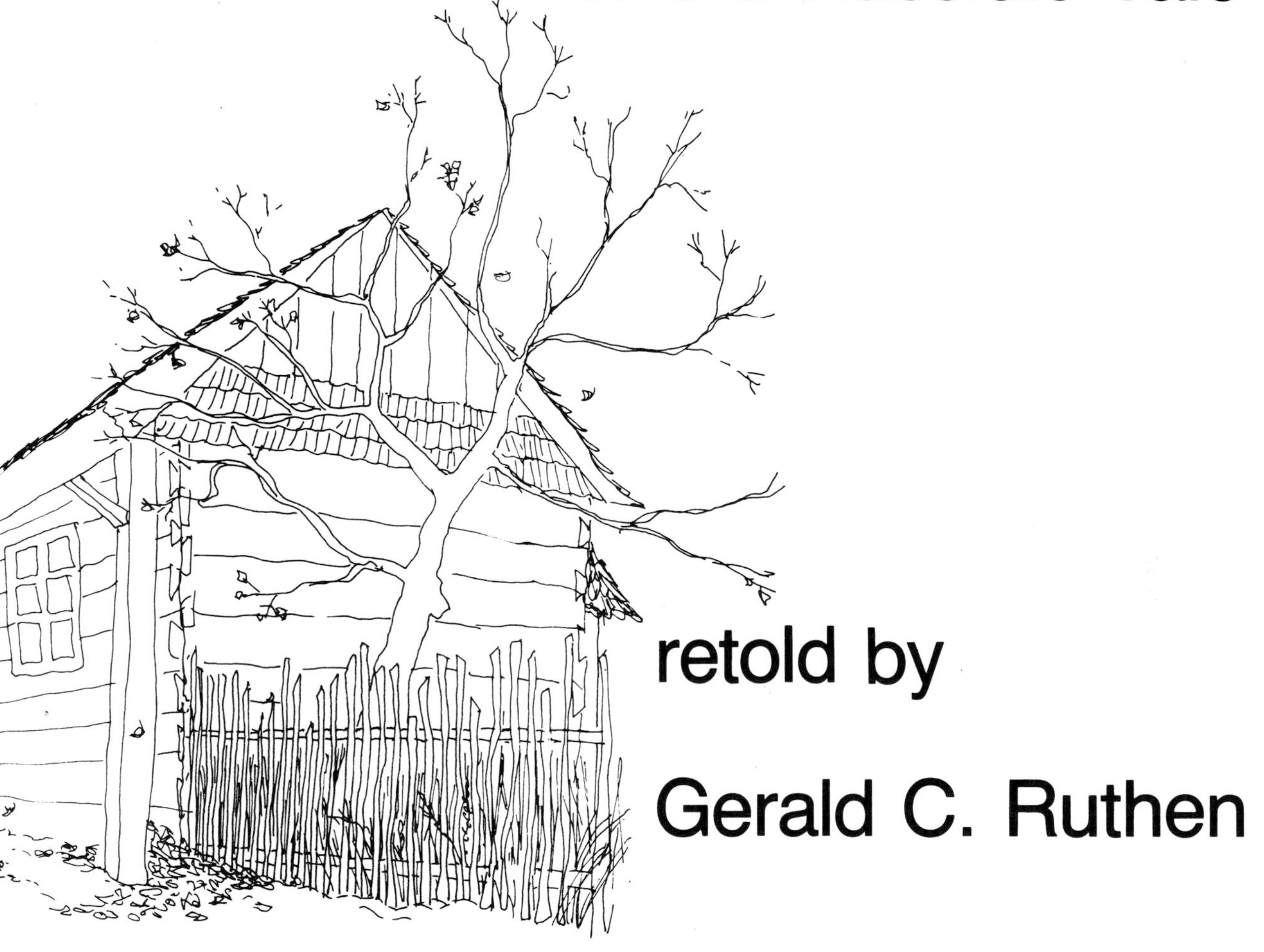

retold by

Gerald C. Ruthen

illustrated by

Marlene L. Ruthen

Manufactured in the United States of America
ISBN: 0-8381-0716-8

To The Adult Reader

Daniel and The Silver Flute is designed for the young child, in terms of language and illustration. It can be read to (with) the child or read by the child him/herself. Its message is two-fold: there are many ways to communicate religious sentiments and anyone can pray—in some mode. Too, it seeks to reassure those children, who cannot (yet) pray, that they are not left out of the Jewish community

To Paula and Russell—
Worth, merit and talent are not always obvious.

Long ago, and far away, in a little village in Central Europe, there lived a boy named Daniel. He was fair of face, and kind and gentle, but, alas he did not learn easily.

Although he tried he did not speak well, he did not read well and, in fact, his family despaired of his ever learning his letters.

His family tried to help him, his friends tried to help him, his neighbors tried to help him. Even the rabbi tried . . . and tried . . . and tried, but Daniel just could not speak clearly, and could not read. Everyone tried, and Daniel tried the hardest, but it was no use.

There were, however, things that Daniel did very well. He tended the sheep for his father, he brought water from the town pump and wood from the woodpile for his mother, and helped his brothers and sisters with many tasks around the house.

There was one other thing that Daniel did often, not very well, mind you, but often—and he did it with all his heart. Daniel played on a shiny silver flute that was a *Hanukkah* present from his grandparents.

The flute went everywhere with Daniel. It went with him to tend the sheep. It went with him to the woodpile. It went with him to *cheder*. It even went to bed with him.

Whenever Daniel was feeling sad, or lonely, or tired, he would take out his little flute and play a little tune. You might not recognize it as a tune, but Daniel knew it was his tune, and it made him feel better.

Daniel felt particularly sad when he went to synagogue with his parents and brothers and sisters. No matter how hard he tried, he could not read the *siddur* as the other boys and girls did and he could not even say clearly the short prayer he had tried to memorize.

And when the cantor led the congregation in the singing, Daniel would try as hard as he could to sing along, but somehow he could not quite say the words, and he could not quite carry the tune.

After the service, Daniel would go around to the back of the house, sit under a big tree, and play his little tune on his silver flute. After a little while, he would feel much better.

Year after year Daniel tried, but he was just not able to sing the songs and read the prayers like the others. As the time for his *Bar Mitzvah* approached, a learned rabbi came to lead the service on the High Holidays at Daniel's synagogue. Daniel's father, who had not taken Daniel to synagogue on *Yom Kippur* before, took him along this time. For although his father was concerned that Daniel might disturb the solemn *Yom Kippur* service, he was more afraid that Daniel might forget he was now supposed to fast, and might eat something. By taking Daniel along, his father could keep an eye on him.

After about an hour of being at services, Daniel began to get restless. Everyone was praying so hard—his brothers and sisters, his mother, his father, the whole congregation and especially the rabbi. But though Daniel tried, he just could not follow the words or sing the songs.

Reaching into his pocket he started to take out his little silver flute, but his father gave him such a look that he put it away quickly.

Another hour passed and the service went on and on. Daniel did not mind that he was hungry and had not eaten since the afternoon before, but he was upset that he could not join in the service. Again he started to take out his flute, but again his father's glance stopped him.

After some time, the rabbi, who had noticed Daniel's unsuccessful efforts to be part of the service, began the *ne'ilah*, the concluding service. He asked God to forgive all those in the congregation who truly in their hearts, wished to atone for past mistakes.

At this moment, Daniel could bear it no more. He, too, wanted to reach God. He, too, wanted to be part of the service. He pulled out his little silver flute and blew a great, loud, but very beautiful note.

Everyone stopped. Everyone looked around. Where had this sound come from? And on *Yom Kippur!* Daniel knew of course. His brothers and sisters guessed. His parents looked rather embarrassed.

But the rabbi had seen Daniel blow that beautiful note on his flute, and a big smile creased his face. The rabbi cut the final prayer short and then stopped. Looking at Daniel he said, "We Jews believe that each of us may pray in his or her own way. And if a prayer comes from the heart, it does not matter to God if it comes in words, or if it comes in song, or even if it comes through the sound of a flute."

The rabbi turned to the congregation and said, "Each of us is important in his own, but different way. I am important for what I am, you each are important for what you are, and Daniel is important for what he is. And each of us, though different, each counts equally. The note that Daniel played on his flute comes from his heart and God understands that it was a prayer and it may be that all our prayers were accepted because Daniel tried so hard. Daniel's prayer is acceptable to God, and, so, certainly we accept it too."

And the kindly rabbi smiled. And the congregation was glad. And Daniel's mother and father and brothers and sisters were very happy.

Daniel hugged his flute, looked around at all the people beaming at him, and for the first time in all the years he had been coming to the synagogue, he was truly content.